Forex and Currency Trading Explained for Beginners

Roggie Clark

Continue Learning At Our Website: Roggieclarkbooks.com

Continue exploring educational resources, tools, books, workbooks, and learning materials designed to help readers continue building knowledge and practical skills. Visit: www.roggieclarkbooks.com

Inside you'll find:

- Educational worksheets
- Beginner-friendly guides
- Printable activities
- Companion materials for books and courses

A growing library of educational content for readers, collectors, learners, parents, teachers, and lifelong students.

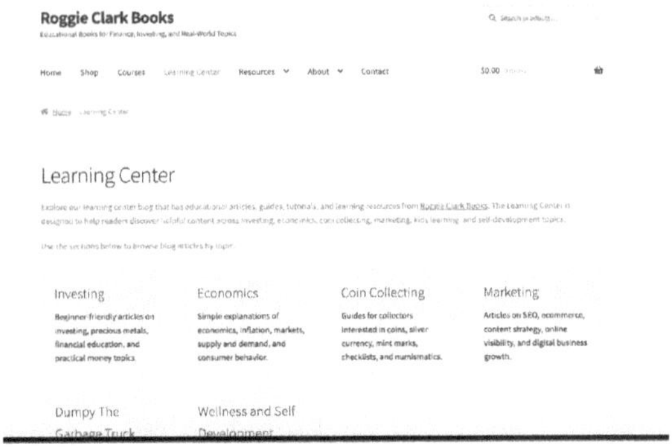

The Strategic Guide to U.S. Mint Gold and Silver Coin Investing

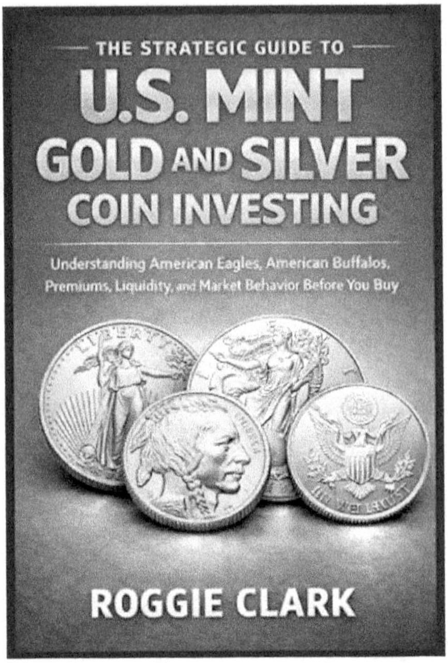

Rather than offering a general introduction to precious metals, this guide examines how American Gold Eagles, American Gold Buffalos, and Silver American Eagles behave in real investor markets.

https://www.amazon.com/Strategic-Guide-U-S-Silver-Investing/dp/B0GQKJF9K6

Copyright

Title: Forex and Currency Trading Explained for Beginners
Author: Roggie Clark

Cover Design: Roggie Clark
Editing: Renee' Clark

Printed in the United States of America

Disclaimer

The views and opinions expressed in this publication are those of the author and do not necessarily reflect the official policies, positions, opinions, or viewpoints of any individual, company, organization, institution, agency, or entity referenced or mentioned within this work.

The author is not necessarily affiliated with, endorsed by, sponsored by, or compensated by any individuals, companies, organizations, brands, institutions, products, or services referenced within this publication unless specifically stated otherwise. Any examples, sample situations, stories, illustrations, or scenarios presented may be fictionalized or simplified for educational purposes. Any resemblance to actual persons, living or dead, businesses, or events is purely coincidental unless otherwise stated.

The information, ideas, strategies, concepts, techniques, opinions, suggestions, and educational materials contained in this publication are provided on an "as is" basis without warranties of any kind, either express or implied. While every effort has been made to provide accurate and current information, neither the author nor the publisher makes any representations or warranties regarding the completeness, accuracy, reliability, suitability, or applicability of the information presented.

This publication is intended solely for educational and informational purposes and should not be interpreted as professional advice of any kind, including but not limited to financial, investment, legal, tax, business, medical, mental health, educational, psychological, or other professional guidance. Readers should conduct their own independent research and consult appropriately qualified professionals before making decisions that may affect their finances, health, business, education, legal matters, personal circumstances, or other important areas of life.

Results, outcomes, and experiences may vary significantly among individuals. Neither the author nor the publisher guarantees any specific outcomes, results, earnings, performance improvements, personal achievements, or benefits resulting from the use of information contained in this publication.

By reading, accessing, or using this publication, you acknowledge and agree that the author and publisher shall not be held liable for any direct, indirect, incidental, consequential, financial, personal, emotional, or other damages, losses, or claims arising from the use, misuse, interpretation, or application of information contained within this publication. You assume full responsibility for any actions, decisions, and outcomes resulting from the use of this material.

Image Credits and Public Domain Notice

All images, illustrations, graphics, photographs, visual references, and related materials included in this publication are believed to be in the public domain, used under applicable licenses or permissions, created by the author or publisher, or obtained from sources that clearly identify them as available for lawful use.

The author and publisher have made a good faith effort to use only visual materials that are lawfully available for use and distribution. Where applicable, images and visual materials may have been resized, cropped, edited, enhanced, stylized, modified, reformatted, or arranged for educational, informational, design, formatting, or presentation purposes.

This publication is intended for educational, informational, and illustrative purposes only. The inclusion of any image, artwork, photograph, visual reference, symbol, historical material, design, or graphic element is not intended to claim ownership over public domain materials or any third-party intellectual property rights that remain with their respective owners.

If you believe any image or visual material included in this publication has been used in error, please contact the author or publisher so the matter may be reviewed and corrected in future editions or releases if necessary.

Any factual information, specifications, historical references, values, descriptions, statistics, or related content accompanying visual materials are provided for general informational purposes only and may change over time. Readers should conduct their own independent research and consult appropriate sources or qualified professionals when making decisions based on information presented in this publication.

This publication is independently produced and is not affiliated with, endorsed by, sponsored by, or associated with any company, organization, government agency, institution, trademark holder, or third party unless specifically stated otherwise.

Table of Contents

Introduction

Forex and currency trading can seem complicated when you first encounter it. Trading platforms display constantly changing prices, currencies are presented in pairs, and beginners quickly encounter unfamiliar terms such as pips, spreads, lots, leverage, margin, liquidity, and volatility. Yet beneath all of that terminology is a relatively simple idea: the foreign exchange market allows one currency to be exchanged for another. Learning how that market operates, why people participate in it, and how forex trades actually work can provide the foundation you need before moving into more advanced trading concepts. This book is designed to build that foundation gradually, beginning with the market itself rather than assuming you already understand how currency trading works.

Understanding Forex and Currency Trading

Forex, short for foreign exchange, refers to the exchange of one currency for another.

Currency exchange happens every day for reasons that have nothing to do with speculative trading.

A traveler from the United States visiting another country may exchange U.S. dollars for the local currency. A business importing products from an overseas supplier may need to make a payment in another currency. An international company may earn revenue in several currencies and eventually convert those earnings back into its home currency.

Banks, governments, investors, financial institutions, and other organizations also exchange currencies for different purposes.

Together, these transactions form the broader **foreign exchange market**, often called the forex market or FX market.

Unlike a traditional stock exchange that operates from a particular centralized marketplace, forex trading takes place through a global network of banks, financial institutions, brokers, businesses, governments, and other market participants.

Currencies are exchanged across different financial centers around the world, allowing forex activity to continue throughout much of the working week.

For beginners, one of the most important concepts to understand is that forex always involves a relationship between two currencies.

If you exchange U.S. dollars for euros, you are not simply "buying euros."

You are exchanging one currency for another.

Forex trading represents this relationship through currency pairs.

For example, EUR/USD represents the euro and the U.S. dollar.

GBP/USD represents the British pound and the U.S. dollar.

USD/JPY represents the U.S. dollar and the Japanese yen.

We will examine exactly how these pairs work later in the book. For now, the important idea is that the price of a currency in forex is expressed relative to another currency.

This price relationship is the **exchange rate**.

Suppose one euro can hypothetically be exchanged for 1.10 U.S. dollars. The exchange rate tells us the relative value of the euro compared with the dollar at that moment.

If the exchange rate changes, the relationship between the currencies has changed.

Forex traders attempt to participate in these changing relationships.

A trader may believe one currency will strengthen relative to another and establish a position based on that expectation. Another trader may believe the opposite.

If the exchange rate moves in the trader's anticipated direction, the position may become profitable. If it moves against the trader, the position may produce a loss.

This sounds straightforward, but currency prices can change for many reasons.

Economic conditions can influence them.

Interest rates can matter.

Central bank decisions can affect expectations.

International trade and investment can influence demand for currencies.

Political developments, market sentiment, unexpected events, and changing expectations can also contribute to currency movements.

Forex trading is therefore not simply a matter of choosing whether a price will move up or down.

Traders are participating in a global market containing enormous numbers of buyers and sellers with different motivations.

Understanding that market is the first step toward understanding the trades taking place within it.

Why People Participate in the Foreign Exchange Market

Not everyone participating in foreign exchange is a forex trader.

This distinction is important because the forex market exists primarily because currencies serve real economic purposes.

Businesses are one major group of participants.

Imagine an American company importing equipment from a European manufacturer. The manufacturer wants to be paid in euros, but the American business primarily earns revenue in dollars.

Somewhere within that transaction, currencies may need to be exchanged.

Now imagine a European company purchasing products from an American supplier.

The currency requirement may move in the opposite direction.

International commerce creates continuous demand for currency conversion.

Multinational businesses can have even more complicated needs.

A company may operate stores in several countries, purchase materials from suppliers located elsewhere, pay employees in multiple currencies, and report its financial results in one home currency.

Changing exchange rates can affect how much its international revenue and expenses are worth.

Some businesses therefore participate in forex markets to manage **currency risk**, which is the possibility that changes in exchange rates will affect the value or cost of an international transaction.

One method businesses may use is **hedging**.

Currency hedging involves attempting to reduce exposure to unfavorable exchange-rate movements. Rather than trying to predict currencies purely for profit, a company may hedge because it wants greater certainty about a future payment or receipt.

Banks and other financial institutions are also major participants.

They may exchange currencies on behalf of customers, facilitate international transactions, manage their own currency exposures, or participate in financial markets for other purposes.

Governments and central banks can participate as well.

Central banks may hold **foreign exchange reserves**, which are assets denominated in foreign currencies and held as part of a country's reserves.

Central banks can also influence currency markets through monetary policy and, under certain circumstances, direct market activity.

Investors create another source of currency transactions.

Suppose an investor in one country wants to purchase bonds, stocks, real estate, or other assets in another country.

The investment may require currency conversion.

When investors move large amounts of capital between countries, these transactions can contribute to demand for different currencies.

Then there are speculators.

Speculation involves taking financial risk based on an expectation about future price movements.

A forex trader who believes one currency will appreciate against another may establish a position designed to benefit if that expectation proves correct.

Another trader may expect the same currency to depreciate.

Unlike a company exchanging currencies because it needs to pay an overseas supplier, the speculative trader may have no underlying commercial need for either currency.

The objective is the price movement itself.

Retail forex traders belong to this broader speculative portion of the market.

Technology and online brokers have made it possible for individuals to access currency trading platforms that were once primarily associated with banks and professional financial institutions.

However, easier access does not make forex trading easy.

The same market that provides opportunities for gains also creates the possibility of substantial losses.

This becomes particularly important because many forex products allow traders to use leverage, which we will explore in Chapter 3.

For now, beginners should recognize that the forex market contains participants with very different objectives.

A business might want certainty.

A bank might be facilitating a customer's transaction.

An international investor may be purchasing foreign assets.

A central bank may be managing reserves or influencing financial conditions.

A retail trader may be attempting to profit from an exchange-rate movement.

All of them can contribute to activity in the same currency market.

Understanding these motivations helps explain why currencies are constantly being bought and sold even when individual traders are not actively speculating.

What Beginners Should Know Before Getting Started

The accessibility of online forex trading can create the impression that getting started simply means opening an account, choosing a currency pair, and deciding whether the price will rise or fall.

There is much more to understand first.

A beginner should know what is actually being traded.

You should understand how a currency pair is quoted, what causes the value of a position to change, and how trading costs can affect the outcome.

You should also understand terminology such as pips, spreads, lots, leverage, margin, and position size before those concepts become real financial commitments.

One of the most important principles is that **trading involves risk**.

There is no forex strategy that guarantees profits.

A currency can move against your expectations even when your reasoning appears logical. Economic data can surprise markets. Central banks can make unexpected decisions. Political or geopolitical developments can rapidly change sentiment.

Sometimes markets simply behave differently from what a trader anticipated.

Leverage can make this uncertainty even more consequential.

A leveraged position allows a trader to control an exposure larger than the amount of money committed as margin. This can make relatively small exchange-rate movements financially significant.

Leverage does not only magnify potential gains.

It can magnify losses as well.

That is why beginners should learn the mechanics before becoming focused on potential returns.

Another important distinction is between learning about forex and being prepared to risk money trading forex.

Those are not the same thing.

You can study how currency pairs work.

You can learn trading terminology.

You can observe price charts.

You can follow economic news.

You can study different approaches to market analysis.

None of those activities requires immediately placing a live trade.

Many beginners use a **demo account**, which allows them to practice with simulated funds rather than real money.

A demo environment can help someone learn how a trading platform works, how orders are entered, how positions change as prices move, and how basic trade management functions operate.

However, simulated trading also has limitations.

Losing simulated money does not necessarily produce the same emotional response as losing actual money. A trader may take risks in a demo account that they would never accept with real funds.

Demo trading should therefore be treated as an educational tool rather than proof that someone will be successful when real money is involved.

Beginners should also be cautious about unrealistic claims surrounding forex.

Currency trading is sometimes promoted online through images of wealth, unusually large returns, expensive lifestyles, or claims that a simple strategy can consistently produce easy income.

That marketing can create unrealistic expectations.

Profitable trading is not guaranteed, and the possibility of loss should be taken seriously.

This makes **risk management** one of the most important subjects a beginner can learn.

Risk management involves deciding how much capital you are willing to expose, how much you are prepared to lose on a particular trade, and how you will respond when the market moves against you.

It also involves understanding that protecting capital can be just as important as identifying potential opportunities.

Trading discipline matters for similar reasons.

A trader who understands the market mechanically can still make poor decisions because of fear, greed, impatience, overconfidence, or frustration.

Someone may increase a position after a loss because they desperately want to recover the money.

Another trader may abandon a plan because a price begins moving quickly.

Someone experiencing several successful trades may become overconfident and begin taking increasingly large risks.

This is why learning forex involves more than terminology and charts.

It also involves developing realistic expectations about uncertainty and your own decision-making.

Throughout this book, we will build that understanding in stages.

First, we will examine how the global foreign exchange market operates and who participates in it.

Then we will look more closely at currency pairs and exchange rates.

From there, we will explain pips, spreads, lots, leverage, and margin before examining how forex orders and positions actually work.

We will then introduce fundamental and technical analysis before ending with risk management and beginner trading practices.

The objective is not to give you a shortcut to forex profits.

It is to help you understand what you are doing before you decide whether and how you want to participate.

Last Thoughts

Forex trading becomes easier to understand once you recognize that it exists within a much larger foreign exchange market. Businesses exchange currencies to conduct international commerce, investors move money between countries, financial institutions facilitate transactions, central banks manage monetary and reserve-related responsibilities, and speculators attempt to profit from changing exchange rates. Retail traders represent only one part of that broader system. Before risking money, beginners should understand the mechanics of currency trading, the terminology they will encounter, the role of leverage, and the possibility of financial loss. Building that foundation first can help you approach forex as a financial market that requires education, risk awareness, and discipline rather than as a shortcut to easy profits.

Chapter 1: How the Foreign Exchange Market Works

The foreign exchange market is the global marketplace where currencies are exchanged. Although beginners often encounter forex through an online trading platform, the market extends far beyond retail trading. Banks process international payments, businesses exchange currencies for global commerce, investors move capital between countries, and financial institutions facilitate transactions for clients around the world. Forex also operates differently from many familiar financial markets because trading activity moves between major financial centers as the global business day progresses. Understanding this structure, the participants within it, and the concepts of liquidity and volatility provides important context before learning how individual forex trades work.

Understanding the Global Forex Market

The foreign exchange market is not organized around one physical location.

When people think about financial markets, they may imagine a large stock exchange where buyers and sellers meet through a centralized system. Forex operates differently.

The market is largely **decentralized**, meaning currency trading takes place through an international network rather than through one central exchange.

Banks, financial institutions, brokers, businesses, governments, investors, and other participants can exchange currencies electronically across this network.

This structure is sometimes described as an **over-the-counter market**, or OTC market.

An over-the-counter market allows transactions to occur directly between market participants or through intermediaries rather than requiring every transaction to pass through a single centralized exchange.

For a beginner, this distinction may seem technical, but it helps explain several characteristics of forex.

There is no single worldwide building where all forex trading occurs.

There is no one opening bell for the entire global currency market.

Instead, trading activity moves around the world as different financial centers begin and end their business days.

This allows the forex market to operate approximately 24 hours a day during the standard trading week.

When business activity is ending in one part of the world, financial centers elsewhere may already be active.

The market typically begins its weekly cycle as financial centers in the Asia-Pacific region become active and continues through Asian, European, and North American trading hours before closing for the weekend.

That does not mean every hour of the day provides identical market conditions.

Some periods experience much greater trading activity than others, which we will explore later in this chapter.

Forex also differs from many markets because currencies serve both financial and economic purposes.

A company's stock primarily represents ownership in that particular company.

A currency, however, functions as money within an economy.

People use currencies to purchase goods and services, pay workers, collect revenue, repay debts, save, invest, and conduct international commerce.

The foreign exchange market helps connect these different monetary systems.

Imagine a company in one country purchasing goods from a supplier located in another.

The buyer may earn revenue in its domestic currency while the seller wants to receive payment in a different currency.

The foreign exchange market makes the conversion possible.

International investing creates similar needs.

An investor who wants to purchase an asset denominated in another currency may first need to exchange funds.

Travel can create much smaller versions of the same process.

When a traveler exchanges dollars for euros, pounds, yen, or another currency, they are participating in foreign exchange even though they are not placing a speculative forex trade.

The global forex market brings these different currency needs together.

Retail forex trading is built on top of this broader market.

A retail trader usually accesses forex through a **forex broker**, a company that provides customers with access to currency trading products and a platform through which trades can be placed.

The exact structure of that access can differ between brokers, jurisdictions, and types of forex products.

This makes understanding the product being offered important.

A beginner should not assume that every platform provides forex exposure in exactly the same way.

The prices displayed on a platform can also change extremely quickly.

Currencies respond to transactions and changing market conditions occurring across the world.

A new economic report can affect expectations.

A central bank announcement can influence currencies.

Unexpected political or geopolitical developments can change sentiment.

Large investment flows can alter demand.

Even when no major announcement occurs, ordinary buying and selling continue throughout the global market.

The price you see on a forex platform is therefore a constantly changing representation of the relationship between two currencies.

Understanding that global structure makes the next question particularly important:

Who is actually participating in this market?

Who Participates in the Currency Market

The forex market contains many different types of participants, and they do not all have the same objectives.

One of the most important groups consists of **commercial banks** and other major financial institutions.

Banks facilitate currency transactions for businesses, investors, governments, and other customers. Large institutions may also conduct transactions with one another.

The market in which major banks and financial institutions transact directly with each other is commonly referred to as the **interbank market**.

This institutional activity forms an important part of the global forex system.

Consider a multinational business that needs to convert a large amount of revenue from one currency into another.

Its bank may facilitate the transaction.

Another customer may need a different currency to purchase an international investment.

The bank can facilitate that transaction as well.

When large numbers of institutions are performing these functions across the global economy, significant amounts of currency can change hands.

Businesses are another important group.

As discussed in the Introduction, international companies may need foreign currencies to pay suppliers, workers, lenders, or other business partners.

An American importer purchasing products from another country may need foreign currency.

An exporter receiving foreign currency may eventually want to convert those earnings into dollars.

A multinational corporation may be dealing with many currencies simultaneously.

For these companies, foreign exchange can be a necessary part of doing business rather than a speculative activity.

Some businesses also participate to manage currency risk.

If a company knows it must make a large payment in another currency several months from now, it may be concerned that the exchange rate could move against it before the payment is due.

The company may use financial arrangements designed to reduce that uncertainty.

Institutional investors are another source of forex activity.

Investment funds, pension funds, asset managers, insurance companies, and other investors may purchase assets across multiple countries.

International investing can require currency conversion.

Suppose an investment fund based in the United States decides to purchase assets denominated in another currency.

The fund may need to obtain that currency.

If the investment is later sold and the proceeds are returned to the United States, another currency conversion may occur.

Large investment decisions can therefore contribute to international currency flows.

Central banks and governments also participate in foreign exchange markets.

A central bank may manage foreign exchange reserves, conduct transactions related to monetary responsibilities, or under certain circumstances attempt to influence conditions affecting its currency.

Central banks can also influence currencies without directly buying or selling them.

Changes in interest rates and monetary policy can alter expectations about an economy and influence international investment decisions.

This is one reason forex traders pay close attention to central bank announcements.

Another group consists of **institutional traders and speculators**.

These participants may trade currencies with the objective of benefiting from changes in exchange rates.

Their strategies can vary considerably.

Some may hold positions for relatively short periods.

Others may base decisions on longer-term economic trends.

Some may rely heavily on economic analysis, while others use quantitative models, price data, or combinations of different methods.

Finally, there are retail traders.

A **retail forex trader** is an individual participating in currency trading through a broker or trading provider rather than as a major financial institution.

Retail traders can access markets from computers, phones, and other devices, making forex appear highly accessible.

But accessibility should not be confused with influence.

An individual retail trade is generally tiny compared with the transactions conducted by large banks, multinational companies, investment funds, and institutional market participants.

Retail traders are entering a market shaped by activity much larger than their individual positions.

Recognizing this can help beginners maintain perspective.

The market does not move because one retail trader believes a currency should rise.

The trader is attempting to interpret and participate in a market created by the collective actions of many different participants.

Those participants may also have objectives that have nothing to do with whether they believe a currency is "good" or "bad."

A corporation may sell a currency simply because it needs another currency to pay a supplier.

An investment fund may exchange currencies because it is reallocating investments.

A bank may be executing transactions for clients.

A trader may be speculating on a price movement.

Different motivations can create buying and selling at the same time.

The resulting activity contributes to the market conditions that retail traders ultimately see on their screens.

Forex Trading Sessions, Liquidity, and Volatility

The global nature of forex allows currency trading activity to continue across different time zones.

Rather than thinking about the forex day as one continuous period with identical conditions, traders commonly divide it into major **trading sessions** associated with important financial centers.

These are generally grouped around the Asia-Pacific, European, and North American portions of the global trading day.

You may encounter references to the Sydney, Tokyo, London, and New York sessions.

These labels provide a convenient way to describe when different regions and financial centers are particularly active.

The precise hours a trader sees can depend on time zone, daylight-saving changes, and the platform being used.

The more important concept is that trading activity changes as different financial centers become active.

This brings us to **liquidity**.

Liquidity refers to how easily an asset can generally be bought or sold without the transaction itself causing a substantial change in its market price.

In a highly liquid market, there are typically many buyers and sellers available.

Major currency pairs can experience substantial liquidity because so many participants around the world are exchanging those currencies.

Liquidity can still vary throughout the trading day.

Suppose relatively few major financial centers are active.

Trading activity may be lower.

Later, another major region opens and more banks, businesses, investors, and traders enter the market.

Activity can increase.

One particularly important period occurs when major trading sessions **overlap**.

A session overlap occurs when two major financial centers are active at the same time.

For example, part of the European trading day overlaps with the North American trading day.

With more participants active simultaneously, certain currency pairs may experience greater trading activity.

This does not mean every session overlap will produce a major price movement.

It simply means market participation and liquidity can differ depending on the time of day and currencies involved.

Liquidity is closely connected with the **spread** that traders encounter, although we will examine spreads more closely in Chapter 3.

In general, highly active markets with many buyers and sellers can make it easier for transactions to occur near prevailing market prices.

During periods of reduced liquidity, trading conditions can become different.

Another concept beginners need to understand is volatility.

Volatility describes the degree or speed at which market prices change over a particular period.

A currency pair experiencing small, gradual movements has lower volatility than one experiencing rapid and substantial price changes.

Volatility can create both opportunity and risk.

A trader needs price movement for a speculative position to generate a meaningful gain.

But greater movement also means the market can move against the trader more rapidly.

Imagine a currency pair that normally moves relatively slowly.

An unexpected central bank announcement occurs.

Within a short period, traders and institutions begin rapidly adjusting their positions.

The exchange rate may move significantly as the market attempts to incorporate the new information.

Volatility has increased.

Economic reports can create similar conditions.

Inflation data, employment reports, interest-rate decisions, economic growth figures, and unexpected political or geopolitical developments can all contribute to sudden price movements.

Liquidity and volatility should not be confused.

A market can be highly liquid and still experience substantial volatility.

If an enormous number of participants are actively buying and selling after a major announcement, the market may have plenty of liquidity while prices are changing rapidly.

Likewise, low liquidity can sometimes contribute to sharper movements because fewer transactions may be available at nearby prices.

Beginners should also understand **slippage**.

Slippage occurs when an order is executed at a different price from the price a trader expected.

Suppose a trader attempts to execute an order during an extremely fast market movement.

The price displayed when the trader submits the order may no longer be available by the time the order reaches the market.

The trade may therefore be filled at another available price.

Slippage can sometimes be favorable, but it can also result in a worse execution price.

Fast-moving markets and reduced liquidity can increase this risk.

This is one reason understanding trading sessions matters beyond simply knowing when forex is open.

The time of day can influence how active particular currencies are.

The currencies involved matter too.

A pair involving European currencies may experience different patterns of activity from a pair involving currencies associated primarily with Asian-Pacific markets.

Major economic announcements can temporarily change those normal patterns.

A beginner does not need to memorize every session time before learning anything else about forex.

What matters is understanding the larger principle:

The forex market may operate throughout much of the working week, but market conditions are not constant.

Participation changes.

Liquidity changes.

Volatility changes.

Spreads can change.

The speed at which prices move can change.

Learning to recognize those differences is part of understanding the environment in which a forex trade is being placed.

Last Thoughts

The foreign exchange market is a decentralized global network connecting banks, businesses, investors, governments, central banks, institutions, brokers, and individual traders. Each participant can enter the market for a different reason, from paying an international supplier to managing currency risk or speculating on changing exchange rates. Because financial centers operate across different time zones, forex activity continues throughout much of the working week, but liquidity and volatility can change as different trading sessions open, close, and overlap. Understanding this market structure gives beginners important context for the prices displayed on a trading platform. In the next chapter, we will move from the market itself to the building blocks of forex trading by examining currency pairs and exchange rates.

Chapter 2: Currency Pairs and Exchange Rates

Every forex trade involves two currencies. One currency is being valued in relation to another, which is why forex prices are presented as currency pairs rather than as standalone prices. Understanding how those pairs are constructed is essential before learning how to calculate trade sizes, use leverage, or place orders. Beginners need to know which currency is being bought, which is being sold, how to interpret an exchange rate, and what it means when a currency pair rises or falls. Once these fundamentals become familiar, the numbers displayed on a forex trading platform become much easier to understand.

Base Currencies, Quote Currencies, and Exchange Rates

A forex currency pair is normally represented by two three-letter currency codes separated by a slash or displayed together.

Examples include:

EUR/USD

GBP/USD

USD/JPY

AUD/USD

Each code represents a particular currency.

USD represents the U.S. dollar.

EUR represents the euro.

GBP represents the British pound.

JPY represents the Japanese yen.

AUD represents the Australian dollar.

The placement of these currencies within the pair is important.

The first currency is the base currency, which we introduced earlier.

The second is the quote currency.

Consider EUR/USD.

EUR is the base currency.

USD is the quote currency.

The exchange rate tells you how much of the quote currency is required to purchase one unit of the base currency.

Suppose EUR/USD is trading at a hypothetical exchange rate of 1.1000.

This means one euro is worth approximately 1.10 U.S. dollars.

If EUR/USD rises to 1.1500, one euro is now worth approximately $1.15.

The euro has strengthened relative to the dollar.

If EUR/USD instead falls to 1.0500, one euro is worth approximately $1.05.

The euro has weakened relative to the dollar.

This provides a useful rule for reading currency pairs.

When a currency pair rises, the base currency is strengthening relative to the quote currency.

When a currency pair falls, the base currency is weakening relative to the quote currency.

Now consider USD/JPY.

In this pair, USD is the base currency and JPY is the quote currency.

Suppose USD/JPY is hypothetically trading at 150.00.

That means one U.S. dollar can be exchanged for approximately 150 Japanese yen.

If the pair rises to 155.00, the dollar has strengthened relative to the yen.

If the pair falls to 145.00, the dollar has weakened relative to the yen.

This is why beginners should avoid thinking about a currency as simply going "up" or "down."

The movement is always relative to another currency.

The U.S. dollar could strengthen against the yen while simultaneously weakening against the euro.

Different economic conditions, market expectations, and trading activity can affect each relationship differently.

Currency pairs also help explain what is happening when a forex trader opens a position.

Suppose a trader buys EUR/USD.

The trader is effectively taking a position that benefits if the euro strengthens relative to the U.S. dollar, subject to the structure and costs of the trading product being used.

In simplified terms, the trader is buying the base currency and selling the quote currency.

If the trader sells EUR/USD, the relationship is reversed.

The trader is taking a position designed to benefit if the euro weakens relative to the dollar.

This simultaneous relationship is fundamental to forex trading.

You are never simply trading "the euro."

You are trading the euro relative to another currency.

The same applies to every other pair.

When analyzing GBP/USD, you are examining the British pound relative to the U.S. dollar.

When analyzing USD/JPY, you are examining the U.S. dollar relative to the Japanese yen.

When analyzing EUR/GBP, you are examining the euro relative to the British pound.

This is also why a trader's opinion about one currency does not automatically provide a complete trading idea.

Suppose you believe the U.S. dollar will strengthen.

Against which currency?

Perhaps you believe economic conditions favor the dollar relative to the yen but not relative to the euro.

The second currency matters.

Currency trading is built around these relationships.

Understanding the base and quote currencies allows you to interpret those relationships correctly before you begin considering whether to buy or sell a pair.

Major, Minor, and Other Currency Pairs

Forex traders frequently organize currency pairs into broad categories.

These classifications can help beginners understand which currencies are commonly traded and why different pairs can have different market characteristics.

One of the most familiar categories is **major currency pairs**.

Major pairs involve the U.S. dollar paired with another widely traded major currency.

Common examples include EUR/USD, GBP/USD, USD/JPY, USD/CHF, AUD/USD, USD/CAD, and NZD/USD.

These pairs receive significant attention because they involve currencies associated with large economies and substantial international financial activity.

They also tend to attract considerable trading participation.

Greater participation can contribute to relatively high liquidity, although liquidity still changes according to market conditions and the time of day.

Another category consists of **minor currency pairs**, which are also commonly called cross-currency pairs or crosses.

These pairs combine major currencies without including the U.S. dollar.

EUR/GBP is one example.

EUR/JPY is another.

GBP/JPY is another.

Suppose a trader wants exposure to the relationship between the euro and the British pound.

The trader does not necessarily need to use a pair involving the U.S. dollar.

EUR/GBP allows the two currencies to be compared directly.

Cross pairs can behave differently from major U.S. dollar pairs because the economic relationship being traded is different.

EUR/GBP, for example, may be particularly sensitive to changing conditions and expectations involving the euro area and the United Kingdom.

EUR/JPY connects a different set of economic environments.

The pair a trader selects therefore determines which currency relationship matters most to the position.

Beginners may also encounter the term **exotic currency pair**.

An exotic pair generally combines a major currency with the currency of a smaller, developing, or less frequently traded economy.

The word exotic does not mean the currency itself is unusual or unimportant.

It is primarily a market classification.

These pairs can sometimes have lower trading activity than major currency pairs.

Lower liquidity can contribute to wider spreads and potentially different trading conditions.

Some currencies may also experience greater volatility, particularly during periods of political, financial, or economic uncertainty.

That can increase trading risk.

This is why beginners should not assume that every forex pair behaves the same way.

A currency pair that moves dramatically may appear attractive because it seems to offer greater profit potential.

But larger movements can also create larger and faster losses.

Wider spreads can increase trading costs as well.

Pair selection should therefore involve more than simply finding the currency that appears to be moving the most.

Traders can consider liquidity, volatility, spreads, trading hours, economic conditions, and their own familiarity with the currencies involved.

The currencies themselves can also respond differently to global developments because the economies behind them are different.

Some economies depend heavily on particular exports.

Others have large financial sectors.

Some countries have relatively high interest rates.

Others maintain lower rates.

Different central banks pursue different policies.

Political and economic risks vary between countries.

All of these differences can influence the relationships represented by currency pairs.

This does not mean a beginner needs to study dozens of currencies immediately.

In fact, trying to follow too many pairs can make learning more difficult.

Each additional currency introduces another economy, central bank, set of economic indicators, and collection of potential market influences.

A beginner may find it easier to first become familiar with how a smaller selection of commonly traded pairs behaves.

The objective is not to find the "best" currency pair.

There is no single pair that is automatically appropriate for every trader or every market condition.

The objective is to understand what you are trading.

Know which currencies are involved.

Know the economies those currencies represent.

Understand when those markets tend to be active.

Know the potential trading costs.

And recognize that different pairs can expose you to different types and levels of risk.

Understanding Currency Appreciation and Depreciation

Currency appreciation and depreciation were introduced earlier, but understanding them from the perspective of an actual currency pair is particularly important for forex traders.

Remember that currency appreciation occurs when one currency increases in value relative to another.

Currency depreciation occurs when it decreases in relative value.

Consider EUR/USD again.

Suppose the pair begins at 1.1000 and later rises to 1.1200.

One euro previously purchased approximately $1.10.

It can now purchase approximately $1.12.

The euro has appreciated against the U.S. dollar.

But every currency relationship has two sides.

If the euro appreciated against the dollar, the dollar simultaneously depreciated against the euro.

This can initially feel confusing because forex traders often describe the movement from the perspective of the pair.

They may simply say:

"EUR/USD moved higher."

Economically, however, that movement represents a change in the relative value of both currencies.

Now suppose USD/JPY falls from 150.00 to 147.00.

Because USD is the base currency, a falling USD/JPY exchange rate means the dollar has depreciated relative to the yen.

The yen has appreciated relative to the dollar.

This relationship is important when deciding whether to go long or short, concepts we will examine more closely when discussing trade execution.

For now, consider a simple example.

A trader expects the euro to appreciate against the U.S. dollar.

The trader might buy EUR/USD.

If the pair rises as anticipated, the position could generate a profit before accounting for trading costs and the specific mechanics of the product.

If EUR/USD falls instead, the position could generate a loss.

Now imagine the trader expects the euro to depreciate against the dollar.

The trader may sell EUR/USD.

If the pair falls, the position could benefit.

If the pair rises, the position could lose money.

This ability to potentially trade both rising and falling currency relationships is one of the characteristics that attracts people to forex.

However, it does not make predicting those movements easier.

Currencies appreciate and depreciate for many reasons.

Interest-rate expectations can change.

Economic growth can strengthen or weaken.

Inflation can surprise the market.

Central banks can alter monetary policy.

International investors can move capital between countries.

Political uncertainty can influence confidence.

Changes in global risk sentiment can alter investment behavior.

Supply and demand can shift for multiple reasons simultaneously.

A beginner therefore needs to distinguish between understanding what a price movement means and knowing why it occurred.

If EUR/USD rises, you can immediately determine from the structure of the pair that the euro has strengthened relative to the dollar.

Explaining why it strengthened may require considerably more analysis.

Perhaps economic information from the euro area was stronger than expected.

Perhaps U.S. economic information disappointed investors.

Perhaps expectations for interest rates changed.

Perhaps several factors were involved.

Sometimes a currency can even appreciate after apparently negative news because traders expected something worse.

This is why price movements should be interpreted within context.

Exchange rates can also matter outside speculative trading.

Currency appreciation and depreciation can affect travelers, businesses, investors, importers, and exporters.

Suppose your home currency appreciates before an international trip.

Your money may purchase more of the foreign currency, potentially making certain expenses abroad relatively less costly.

A weaker home currency can have the opposite effect.

Businesses experience similar relationships on a much larger scale.

An importer may face higher costs when its domestic currency depreciates against the currency required to purchase foreign products.

An exporter may benefit in some circumstances because its products become relatively less expensive to foreign buyers.

Multinational companies may see the value of overseas revenue change when those earnings are converted into their reporting currency.

The same exchange rates displayed on a retail forex platform therefore have consequences throughout the real economy.

For traders, appreciation and depreciation represent potential price opportunities and risks.

For businesses and consumers, they can influence real purchasing power and costs.

Both perspectives originate from the same fundamental relationship:

One currency is always being valued relative to another.

Last Thoughts

Currency pairs provide the basic language through which forex prices are expressed. Understanding the base currency and quote currency allows you to determine what an exchange rate means and correctly interpret whether one currency is strengthening or weakening relative to another. Major, minor, and other currency pairs can also have different levels of liquidity, volatility, trading activity, and potential cost, making it important to understand the specific currencies involved rather than treating every pair as interchangeable. Once you can confidently read a currency pair and understand appreciation and depreciation, the next step is learning how those price movements translate into actual trading values. In the next chapter, we will examine pips, spreads, lots, position sizes, leverage, and margin, the mechanics that determine how currency movements can translate into trading gains, losses, costs, and risk.

Chapter 3: Pips, Spreads, Lots, Leverage, and Margin

Once you understand currency pairs and exchange rates, the next step is understanding how changes in those exchange rates translate into an actual forex position. A movement that appears small on a price quote can have a very different financial impact depending on the size of the position, the value of each price movement, the spread charged when entering and exiting the market, and whether leverage is being used. These mechanics are essential for beginners because they determine both potential gains and potential losses. Before placing a forex trade, you should understand what a pip represents, how position sizes are measured, and why leverage and margin can significantly increase trading risk.

Understanding Pips, Bid and Ask Prices, and Spreads

Forex exchange rates can change by very small amounts.

Consider a hypothetical EUR/USD quote moving from:

1.1050

to:

1.1051

The difference appears tiny, but forex traders need a standardized way to describe these small price movements.

A **pip**, short for percentage in point or price interest point, is a standardized unit commonly used to describe changes in a currency pair's exchange rate.

For many currency pairs, one pip corresponds to the fourth decimal place.

For example, suppose EUR/USD moves from 1.1050 to 1.1051.

That is a movement of one pip.

If it moves from 1.1050 to 1.1060, the pair has moved 10 pips.

If it rises from 1.1050 to 1.1100, it has moved 50 pips.

Currency pairs involving the Japanese yen are commonly quoted differently. For many yen pairs, a pip corresponds to the second decimal place.

Suppose USD/JPY moves from 150.25 to 150.26.

That is a one-pip movement.

If it moves from 150.25 to 150.35, that is a 10-pip movement.

Modern forex platforms may display additional decimal places beyond the traditional pip.

For example, EUR/USD might appear as:

1.10503

The final digit represents a fraction of a pip, sometimes called a **pipette** or fractional pip.

A pipette allows price changes to be quoted more precisely.

Knowing how many pips a currency pair moved tells you something about the size of the exchange-rate change, but it does not automatically tell you how much money was gained or lost.

That depends on the position size.

A 20-pip movement on a very small position can have a much smaller financial impact than the same 20-pip movement on a large position.

Before calculating that relationship, beginners also need to understand that forex platforms commonly display two prices rather than one.

These are the **bid price** and **ask price**.

The bid is generally the price at which the trader can sell the base currency through the quoted market.

The ask is generally the price at which the trader can buy the base currency.

The ask is normally higher than the bid.

Suppose EUR/USD is hypothetically quoted as:

Bid: 1.1050

Ask: 1.1052

A trader buying the pair would generally enter at or near the ask price.

A trader selling the pair would generally transact at or near the bid price, subject to execution conditions.

The difference between those two prices is the spread.

We introduced the spread briefly in Chapter 1. Now we can examine what it means for a trade.

In this example:

1.1052 - 1.1050 = 0.0002

For a currency pair where the fourth decimal place represents a pip, this would be a two-pip spread.

The spread is one way trading costs can arise.

Suppose a trader buys EUR/USD at the ask price of 1.1052.

At that same moment, the bid is only 1.1050.

If the trader immediately closed the position under unchanged market conditions, the difference between the entry and exit prices would create a loss associated with the spread.

The market therefore needs to move sufficiently in the trader's favor before the position can overcome that initial difference.

Spreads are not necessarily constant.

They can change according to the currency pair, broker or trading provider, market conditions, and liquidity.

A heavily traded major currency pair may have a relatively narrow spread during active market conditions.

A less liquid pair may have a wider spread.

Spreads can also widen during periods of unusual volatility, reduced liquidity, or major economic announcements.

This is one reason traders should pay attention to more than the direction of a currency pair.

Trading costs can affect the actual result.

Depending on the broker and product being used, traders may encounter additional costs such as commissions or financing charges. These should be understood before trading because the spread is not necessarily the only expense involved.

Pips and spreads provide the foundation for measuring price movement and some trading costs.

To understand what those movements mean financially, we need to introduce position size.

Lots, Position Sizes, and Calculating Trade Exposure

When you place a forex trade, the size of the position matters enormously.

A trader controlling a relatively small amount of currency will experience a different financial result from a trader controlling a much larger amount, even if both trade the same currency pair and experience the exact same price movement.

Forex position sizes have traditionally been described using **lots**.

A standard lot commonly represents 100,000 units of the base currency.

A **mini lot** commonly represents 10,000 units.

A **micro lot** commonly represents 1,000 units.

Some trading platforms may allow other position increments, so beginners should always understand how their specific platform expresses trade size rather than assuming every provider uses identical controls.

Consider EUR/USD.

If a trader establishes a position equivalent to one standard lot, the position represents 100,000 units of the base currency, which in this pair is euros.

A mini-lot position would represent 10,000 euros.

A micro-lot position would represent 1,000 euros.

This brings us to **position size**, which refers to the amount of a currency or financial exposure represented by a trade.

Position size affects the monetary value of each pip movement.

Consider a simplified EUR/USD example where one standard lot represents 100,000 euros.

If one pip equals 0.0001 dollars per euro, then:

100,000 x 0.0001 = $10

Under those simplified conditions, a one-pip movement would correspond to approximately $10 for a one-standard-lot position.

A 10-pip movement would correspond to approximately $100.

A 50-pip movement would correspond to approximately $500.

Now consider a mini lot of 10,000 units.

10,000 x 0.0001 = $1

A one-pip movement would correspond to approximately $1 under the same simplified conditions.

A 50-pip movement would correspond to approximately $50.

With a micro lot of 1,000 units:

1,000 x 0.0001 = $0.10

A 50-pip movement would correspond to approximately $5.

These examples show why saying that a trader "made 50 pips" does not tell you how much money was earned.

The position size matters.

The currency pair matters as well.

Pip values are not always fixed at the same dollar amount. Depending on the currencies involved, the exchange rate, the account currency, and the size of the position, additional calculations may be necessary to determine the monetary value of a pip.

Trading platforms often calculate this information automatically, but beginners should still understand the principle.

A larger position makes each price movement financially larger.

This applies in both directions.

If increasing a position size doubles the potential value of a favorable pip movement, it also doubles the potential impact of an unfavorable movement under otherwise identical conditions.

This is why position size is closely connected to risk management.

Another useful concept is **trade exposure**.

Trade exposure describes the amount of market exposure created by a position.

Suppose a trader has $5,000 in a trading account.

That does not necessarily mean the trader is limited to controlling a $5,000 forex position.

Depending on the product and applicable leverage, the trader may be able to establish exposure much larger than the account balance.

That possibility can initially sound attractive.

A small amount of money appears capable of controlling a much larger position.

But the trader is also exposing the account to price movements based on that larger position.

Understanding this distinction is critical.

Account balance and market exposure are not necessarily the same thing.

A trader with a modest account can create a position large enough that a relatively small adverse currency movement produces a substantial loss.

This is where leverage enters the picture.

How Leverage and Margin Work

Leverage allows a trader to control a market position larger than the amount of capital required to open that position.

It is one of the most important concepts in forex trading because it can dramatically change the financial consequences of relatively small exchange-rate movements.

Suppose a trader wants exposure to a $10,000 position.

Without leverage, controlling that entire position could require approximately $10,000.

Now suppose the trading arrangement provides 10:1 leverage.

In simplified terms, the trader may be able to control $10,000 of exposure with $1,000 of required capital.

At 20:1 leverage, the required amount could be lower still, depending on the product, broker requirements, and applicable regulations.

The amount of money that must be set aside to support a leveraged position is called **margin**.

Margin is not simply a fee paid to place the trade.

It represents capital required in the account to open or maintain the leveraged position.

Suppose a trader wants to control a $20,000 position and the applicable margin requirement is 5 percent.

Five percent of $20,000 is $1,000.

The trader would therefore need approximately $1,000 in required margin for that position under this simplified example.

But this does not mean the trader's financial exposure is only $1,000.

The position is still based on $20,000 of market exposure.

That distinction explains why leverage can become dangerous.

Imagine the $20,000 position moves 1 percent against the trader.

One percent of $20,000 is $200.

Relative to the $20,000 exposure, that movement may appear modest.

Relative to the $1,000 used as margin, however, the $200 loss represents 20 percent of that amount.

If the position moves 2 percent against the trader, the loss would be approximately $400 under the simplified example.

The underlying market moved only 2 percent, but the effect relative to the capital supporting the position is much larger.

Leverage therefore magnifies the financial impact of price movements.

This can magnify gains when the market moves in the trader's favor.

It can magnify losses when the market moves against the trader.

Beginners sometimes focus heavily on the first half of that relationship.

A trader might think:

"If I can control a larger position, I can make more money from a small movement."

That is mathematically possible.

But the complete statement is:

"If I control a larger position, I can gain or lose more money from a small movement."

The market does not reduce the downside simply because leverage was used.

This is why maximum available leverage should not be confused with an appropriate amount of leverage.

A platform may allow a trader to establish a certain position size, but that does not mean using the maximum available exposure is sensible.

Margin creates additional considerations.

As an open position gains or loses value, the amount of usable capital within the account can change.

Used margin refers to the amount currently committed to supporting open leveraged positions.

Free margin generally refers to account funds available beyond the amount being used to maintain those positions, although exact terminology and calculations can vary between platforms.

If losses become sufficiently large, the account may no longer have enough equity to satisfy the broker's margin requirements.

This can lead to a **margin call** or other action required under the broker's rules.

Historically, a margin call could involve a broker asking a customer to deposit additional funds. On modern electronic trading platforms, the process may instead involve warnings, restrictions, or automatic position liquidation when account equity falls below specified thresholds.

A **stop-out** occurs when a broker begins automatically closing positions because the account no longer satisfies required margin levels, depending on the broker's policies and applicable rules.

This can happen quickly in a highly leveraged account.

Suppose a trader opens several large leveraged positions at the same time.

Each position requires margin.

If several trades move against the trader simultaneously, account equity can decline while available margin becomes increasingly limited.

The trader may be forced out of positions before the market has an opportunity to recover.

This demonstrates another risk of leverage:

It reduces the amount of adverse price movement an account may be able to withstand when position sizes become too large relative to available capital.

Different jurisdictions can impose different leverage limits and margin requirements for retail forex products. Brokers can also have their own policies within applicable regulatory requirements.

Beginners should therefore understand the exact terms associated with their trading account rather than relying on a leverage example encountered in a book, video, or online discussion.

Leverage ratios, margin requirements, liquidation procedures, financing costs, and available products can differ.

The principle, however, remains consistent.

Leverage changes the relationship between the capital committed and the market exposure controlled.

The greater that exposure becomes relative to the trader's available capital, the more significant relatively small price movements can become.

This is why leverage should be understood primarily as a risk amplifier rather than simply a way to increase potential profits.

Before entering any leveraged trade, a trader should know the size of the position, the approximate value of relevant price movements, the margin required, and the amount that could be lost if the market moves against the position.

Those calculations transform leverage from an abstract trading feature into something much more important:

A measurable financial risk.

Last Thoughts

Pips, spreads, lots, leverage, and margin turn exchange-rate movements into the practical financial mechanics of forex trading. Pips provide a standardized way to describe price changes, while bid and ask prices create the spread traders encounter when entering and exiting positions. Lots and position sizes determine how financially significant those price movements become. Leverage can then allow a trader to control exposure much larger than the capital committed as margin, magnifying both potential gains and potential losses. Understanding these relationships is essential before placing a forex trade because even a relatively small currency movement can have a substantial effect when position size and leverage are large. In the next chapter, we will build on these mechanics by examining how traders actually enter, manage, and exit forex positions using different types of trading orders.

Chapter 4: Placing and Managing Forex Trades

Understanding currency pairs, pips, spreads, position sizes, leverage, and margin gives you the mechanical foundation needed to understand what happens when a forex trade is actually placed. The next step is learning how traders enter and exit positions. Forex platforms offer different order types that allow traders to buy or sell immediately, request an entry at a particular price, or automatically close a position when certain conditions are reached. Traders also need to understand what it means to go long or short and how trading costs can affect the final result. Learning these mechanics before risking money can help prevent simple order-entry mistakes from becoming costly trading mistakes.

Market, Limit, Stop, and Stop-Loss Orders

A forex trade begins with an **order**.

An order is an instruction to a broker or trading platform to buy or sell according to specified conditions.

Different order types exist because traders do not always want to enter or exit the market in the same way.

Sometimes a trader wants to establish a position immediately.

At other times, the trader wants to wait until the currency pair reaches a particular price.

One of the most straightforward order types is a **market order**.

A market order instructs the trading provider to execute a transaction at the best available price.

Suppose EUR/USD is currently trading near 1.1000 and a trader wants to buy the pair immediately.

The trader could submit a market order.

The order would generally be filled at the best available ask price when the transaction is executed.

However, the price displayed when the trader clicks the button is not always guaranteed to be the exact execution price.

Prices can move quickly.

As we discussed earlier, slippage can occur when the available market price changes between the time an order is submitted and the time it is executed.

This becomes particularly important during periods of high volatility.

A major economic announcement could cause prices to change rapidly, potentially resulting in execution at a price different from what the trader expected.

Market orders prioritize execution rather than guaranteeing a specific price.

A trader who does not want to enter immediately may instead use a **limit order**.

A limit order instructs the trading platform to execute a transaction at a specified price or better, if that price becomes available.

Suppose EUR/USD is trading at 1.1050, but a trader only wants to buy if the pair falls to 1.1000.

Rather than watching the screen continuously, the trader could place a buy limit order around the desired level.

If the market reaches the required conditions, the order may be eligible for execution.

If the price never reaches that level, the trade may never occur.

Limit orders can therefore help traders plan entries instead of feeling pressured to enter at the current market price.

Another type is a **stop order**, sometimes called a stop-entry order when it is being used to establish a new position.

A stop-entry order becomes active when the market reaches a specified price.

Suppose EUR/USD is trading at 1.1000.

A trader believes that a move above 1.1100 would provide a reason to enter a long position.

The trader could place a buy stop above the current market price.

If the pair reaches the specified level, the order may trigger and become eligible for execution.

A sell stop can be used in the opposite direction.

Suppose a trader only wants to sell EUR/USD if the price falls below 1.0900.

A sell stop could be placed around that level.

Limit and stop orders may sound similar because both wait for a specified price before taking action.

The difference lies in what the trader wants to happen.

A limit entry is generally used when the trader wants to transact at a more favorable price than the current market price.

A stop entry is generally used when the trader wants to enter after price moves beyond a specified level.

Another particularly important order type is the **stop-loss order**.

A stop-loss order is designed to close a position if the market reaches a predetermined adverse price level.

Suppose a trader buys EUR/USD at 1.1000.

The trader decides before entering the position that they do not want to remain in the trade if the pair falls substantially below the entry price.

A stop-loss order might be placed at a lower predetermined level.

If the market reaches that level, the order is triggered and the position may be closed.

Stop-loss orders are an important risk-management tool because they allow traders to establish an exit point before emotions become involved.

Without a predetermined exit, a trader facing a losing position may begin making decisions based on hope.

The trader might think:

"Maybe it will come back."

The loss becomes larger.

The trader waits longer.

Eventually, a relatively manageable loss can become significantly more damaging.

A stop loss provides a predefined point at which the original trading idea is no longer allowed to continue exposing the account to additional loss.

However, beginners should understand that a standard stop-loss order does not necessarily guarantee the exact exit price.

During a rapid market movement or a gap in available prices, the position may be executed at the next available price, potentially resulting in slippage.

Different brokers and products may offer different order features, including certain guaranteed stop products under specific conditions and costs. Traders should understand exactly how their platform handles orders rather than assuming every stop operates identically.

Orders are tools.

They do not determine whether the underlying trading idea is correct.

A well-placed order can still produce a losing trade if the market moves against the position.

The purpose of understanding orders is to give the trader greater control over how a trading decision is executed.

Going Long, Going Short, and Closing Positions

Forex traders can potentially participate in both rising and falling currency relationships.

To understand how, we need to distinguish between going long and going short.

A **long position** is a position designed to benefit if the traded market rises.

Suppose a trader believes the euro will appreciate relative to the U.S. dollar.

EUR/USD is currently trading at a hypothetical 1.1000.

The trader decides to buy the pair.

The trader is now long EUR/USD.

If EUR/USD rises to 1.1100, the movement is favorable to the long position.

If it falls to 1.0900, the movement is unfavorable.

Remember what is happening within the currency pair.

Buying EUR/USD means taking a position based on the euro strengthening relative to the dollar.

The trader is not simply betting that "currencies will rise."

The trader is taking a view on the relationship between two particular currencies.

A **short position** is designed to benefit if the traded market falls.

Suppose a trader believes the euro will depreciate against the dollar.

Instead of buying EUR/USD, the trader sells the pair.

The trader is now short EUR/USD.

If EUR/USD falls from 1.1000 to 1.0900, that movement is favorable to the short position.

If the pair rises to 1.1100, the movement is unfavorable.

The ability to go short can initially feel unusual to beginners who are familiar with the idea of buying an asset first and selling it later.

Forex is different because each pair already contains a buying and selling relationship.

When you buy one currency in the pair, you are simultaneously taking the opposite side relative to the other.

This makes both upward and downward exchange-rate movements potentially tradable.

But it also creates risk in either direction.

The fact that a trader can potentially profit when a currency pair falls does not mean falling markets are easier to predict.

A short position can lose money just as quickly as a long position when the market moves against the trader.

Every open trade eventually needs to be closed.

Closing a position involves taking the opposite transaction from the one used to open it.

If a trader opened a position by buying EUR/USD, closing it generally involves selling the corresponding position.

If the trader opened by selling EUR/USD, closing generally involves buying it back.

The difference between the opening and closing prices contributes to the trade's profit or loss.

A trader can close a position manually.

The position can also be closed through an order placed in advance.

We have already discussed stop-loss orders, which can close a trade when the market moves adversely.

Traders may also use a **take-profit order**.

A take-profit order is designed to close a position when the market reaches a predetermined favorable price level.

Suppose a trader buys EUR/USD at 1.1000 and believes 1.1150 represents an appropriate profit objective.

The trader could place a take-profit order around that level.

If the market reaches the specified price and the order is executed, the position closes.

This allows the trader to define a potential exit without continuously watching the market.

Using predefined exits can also help create structure.

Before entering, a trader can consider:

Where will I exit if the trade is wrong?

Where might I exit if the trade moves in my favor?

How much am I risking between my entry and stop?

How much potential movement exists between my entry and target?

This relationship introduces the concept of **risk-reward ratio**.

A risk-reward ratio compares the amount a trader is prepared to risk with the potential reward being targeted.

Suppose a trader is willing to risk $50 on a trade while targeting a potential $100 gain.

The potential reward is twice the amount being risked.

This would commonly be described as risking one unit in pursuit of two units of potential reward.

Risk-reward analysis does not tell you whether the trade will succeed.

A trade with a large potential reward may have a relatively low probability of reaching its target.

A trade with a smaller target may have a higher probability but provide less potential reward.

The concept simply helps traders think about the relationship between what they could lose and what they hope to gain before entering a position.

This is much more useful than deciding how much to risk after the market has already moved against you.

Understanding Profit, Loss, and Trading Costs

A forex position becomes profitable or unprofitable as the exchange rate moves relative to the trader's entry price.

The basic relationship is straightforward.

If a trader is long and the market rises sufficiently above the entry price, the position can generate a profit.

If the market falls, the position can generate a loss.

For a short position, the relationship is reversed.

But calculating the actual result requires more than simply looking at whether the price moved up or down.

Position size matters.

Pip value matters.

The entry and exit prices matter.

Trading costs matter.

Leverage affects the amount of exposure relative to the capital supporting the position.

Consider a simplified example.

A trader buys EUR/USD at 1.1000.

The pair later rises to 1.1050.

That represents a 50-pip favorable movement under a traditional four-decimal pip convention.

If the trader's position has an approximate pip value of $1, the price movement would represent approximately $50 before applicable trading costs.

If the pip value were $10 instead, the same 50-pip movement would represent approximately $500 before costs.

The currency pair moved exactly the same distance.

The position size changed the financial result.

Now suppose the pair moves 50 pips against the trader.

The same relationship applies to the loss.

A larger position increases the financial impact of both favorable and unfavorable movements.

This is why traders should know their potential monetary exposure before entering.

It is easier to think rationally about a hypothetical loss before the trade exists than after watching money disappear from an account.

Trading costs also reduce the amount a trader ultimately keeps from profitable positions and increase the burden that must be overcome for a trade to become profitable.

We have already discussed spreads.

The spread creates a difference between the price at which a trader can buy and the price at which the trader can sell.

Depending on the trading arrangement, a broker may also charge a **commission**, which is a direct fee associated with executing a trade.

Some providers may rely more heavily on spreads.

Others may offer narrower quoted spreads while charging separate commissions.

The structure varies.

Another potential expense is an **overnight financing charge**, sometimes referred to in forex contexts as a swap or rollover charge.

When certain leveraged forex positions remain open beyond a specified daily cutoff, the trader may pay or, under some circumstances, receive an amount associated with the currencies, interest-rate conditions, and the broker's pricing structure.

The exact calculation can vary significantly.

A beginner planning to hold positions for multiple days should therefore understand the financing terms associated with the trading product.

A trade that appears profitable based solely on the difference between entry and exit prices may produce a somewhat different result after spreads, commissions, financing charges, and other applicable costs are included.

This distinction becomes particularly important for traders attempting to capture very small price movements.

Suppose a strategy aims to make only a few pips per trade.

If the spread and other transaction costs consume a significant portion of that movement, the strategy needs to overcome those expenses repeatedly before generating a net profit.

Frequent trading can therefore create substantial cumulative costs even when the cost of each individual transaction appears small.

Traders should think in terms of **net profit or loss**, meaning the result after applicable trading costs rather than simply the gross movement of the position.

This provides a more realistic picture of performance.

Profit and loss also affect account equity.

Suppose an account begins with $5,000.

If closed trades produce a combined net loss of $500, the account has lost 10 percent of its starting capital.

Recovering from that loss requires more than simply earning 10 percent on the remaining balance.

After falling from $5,000 to $4,500, the trader would need to earn approximately 11.1 percent on the remaining $4,500 to return to $5,000.

Larger losses make recovery increasingly difficult.

A 50 percent loss requires a 100 percent gain on the remaining capital merely to return to the original balance.

This is one reason controlling losses is so important.

Traders sometimes become overly focused on how much money a successful trade could make.

A more disciplined question is:

How much could this trade cost me if I am wrong?

The answer should include more than the expected price movement.

Consider the position size.

Consider leverage.

Consider the stop-loss level.

Consider the spread.

Consider commissions or financing costs when applicable.

Consider whether volatility or slippage could affect execution.

Then decide whether the potential loss is acceptable before entering the position.

This approach does not prevent losing trades.

Losses are part of trading.

What it can do is help prevent a single trading decision from creating a level of damage that the trader never intended to accept.

Last Thoughts

Placing a forex trade involves more than clicking a buy or sell button. Market, limit, stop, and stop-loss orders give traders different ways to control when positions are entered and exited, while long and short positions allow traders to take views on both rising and falling currency relationships. The final outcome of a trade depends on the entry price, exit price, position size, pip value, and applicable trading costs, not simply whether the trader correctly anticipated the general direction of the market. Learning these mechanics can help beginners plan trades before money is at risk rather than making important decisions after a position is already open. In the next chapter, we will move from executing trades to analyzing potential opportunities by examining fundamental analysis, technical analysis, trends, support and resistance, and the role of a trading plan.

Chapter 5: Analyzing the Forex Market

Placing a forex trade explains how a position enters the market, but it does not explain why a trader might choose that position in the first place. Traders use different forms of market analysis to develop an opinion about how a currency pair may behave. Two of the most common approaches are fundamental analysis, which focuses on economic and financial conditions, and technical analysis, which focuses on price behavior and charts. Neither approach can predict currency movements with certainty. Instead, analysis provides a structured way to evaluate market conditions, identify potential opportunities, and decide whether a particular trade fits within a broader trading plan.

Fundamental Analysis and Economic News

Fundamental analysis was introduced earlier as a way of evaluating the economic forces that may influence currencies.

For forex traders, **fundamental analysis** can involve studying economic growth, inflation, employment, interest rates, central bank policy, international trade, and other conditions that may affect the relative demand for currencies.

The key word is relative.

Remember that every currency pair contains two currencies.

A trader analyzing EUR/USD is not only interested in economic conditions affecting the euro. Conditions affecting the U.S. dollar matter as well.

Suppose economic growth is strengthening in the euro area while weakening in the United States.

That difference could potentially influence expectations surrounding EUR/USD.

But growth alone does not determine the exchange rate.

Inflation might be moving differently.

Interest rates may differ.

Central banks may be pursuing different policies.

Investors may already expect the growth difference.

A fundamental trader therefore attempts to combine several pieces of economic information into a broader view.

Interest rates receive considerable attention because they can influence borrowing, saving, investment, and international capital flows.

If traders believe one central bank will raise interest rates while another is expected to lower them, the difference between those expected policies may influence the relative attractiveness of the currencies.

However, traders are often interested in future policy rather than simply today's interest rate.

This is where economic news becomes particularly important.

Governments, statistical agencies, central banks, and other institutions regularly release economic information.

Traders may monitor reports involving inflation, employment, economic growth, consumer activity, business conditions, and other areas of the economy.

An economic calendar, introduced earlier, helps organize when many of these scheduled releases are expected to occur.

Beginners may encounter economic calendars that classify events according to their expected market importance.

A major central bank decision or widely followed inflation report might be identified as a high-impact event.

A less closely watched report may receive a lower classification.

These classifications can be useful, but they do not guarantee how much the market will move.

A supposedly important event can produce little movement if the result matches expectations.

Another event can produce a larger reaction if the information significantly surprises market participants.

This is because forex markets respond not only to economic conditions but also to expectations.

Suppose the market expects an inflation report to show 3 percent inflation.

The actual result is 3 percent.

Even if 3 percent is economically significant, the report may contain relatively little new information because participants were already expecting it.

Now suppose the result is 4 percent.

That difference could force traders to reconsider their assumptions about inflation and future monetary policy.

The actual number matters, but the difference between expectations and reality can matter just as much.

This is why beginners should avoid automatically interpreting economic reports as simply positive or negative.

Consider an employment report.

Strong job creation might appear positive for a currency because it can indicate a healthy economy.

But suppose employment is so strong that traders become concerned about inflation.

The report could increase expectations for higher interest rates.

That adds another potential currency effect.

Now imagine the economy is already experiencing very high inflation and policymakers are concerned that restrictive monetary policy is damaging economic growth.

The same employment report exists within a different economic environment.

Context changes interpretation.

Central bank announcements can be especially important because policymakers influence interest rates and monetary conditions.

Traders may pay attention to the actual interest-rate decision, the accompanying policy statement, economic projections, and comments made during speeches or press conferences.

Sometimes a central bank leaves interest rates unchanged while changing its language about the future.

That change in communication can influence currencies because traders adjust their expectations.

A central bank that appears increasingly concerned about inflation may be described as **hawkish**.

A hawkish policy stance generally emphasizes controlling inflation and may be associated with tighter monetary policy.

A central bank that places greater emphasis on supporting economic activity or reducing restrictive monetary conditions may be described as **dovish**.

These terms describe general policy attitudes rather than guaranteed future actions.

A central bank can also change its stance as economic conditions change.

Fundamental traders therefore need to update their analysis rather than assuming that yesterday's economic story will remain valid indefinitely.

Economic news can also create significant short-term volatility.

A trader may have a reasonable long-term fundamental view but still experience a rapid adverse movement when unexpected information reaches the market.

This is another reason analysis cannot replace risk management.

Fundamental analysis helps explain possible reasons for currency movements.

It does not guarantee that a particular currency will move in the direction a trader expects or within the timeframe the trader expects.

Technical Analysis, Trends, Support, and Resistance

Fundamental analysis examines the economic environment surrounding currencies.

Technical analysis approaches the market from a different perspective.

Technical analysis involves studying historical price behavior and other market data in an attempt to identify patterns, trends, levels, or conditions that may help inform trading decisions.

A technical trader may use a price chart as the primary source of information.

Forex charts can display price behavior over different periods.

A trader could examine very short-term movements or study price changes occurring over days, weeks, or months.

The period represented by each price bar or candle is called a **timeframe**.

For example, a one-hour chart may organize price behavior into one-hour intervals.

A daily chart organizes the information into daily periods.

Different timeframes can show very different perspectives of the same currency pair.

A movement that appears dramatic on a short-term chart may look relatively insignificant when viewed over several months.

This is why traders should understand the timeframe they are analyzing.

One of the most basic concepts in technical analysis is a **trend**.

A trend describes the general direction in which a market has been moving.

An uptrend generally consists of prices moving progressively higher over time.

A downtrend generally involves prices moving progressively lower.

A market that is not developing a clear upward or downward direction may be described as moving sideways or ranging.

Traders sometimes attempt to identify trends because they want to understand the market's broader direction before deciding how to approach a trade.

Suppose a currency pair has been producing a series of higher highs and higher lows.

A technical trader might interpret that structure as evidence of an uptrend.

If the pair instead produces lower highs and lower lows, the trader may view the market as being in a downtrend.

Trends do not continue forever.

A currency pair can reverse, consolidate, or transition into a different market environment.

Technical traders therefore use additional concepts to evaluate where price may encounter buying or selling activity.

Two common concepts are **support** and **resistance**.

Support refers to a price area where buying interest has previously been sufficient to slow or reverse a decline.

Resistance refers to an area where selling activity has previously been sufficient to slow or reverse an advance.

Suppose a currency pair repeatedly falls toward 1.1000 and then begins rising.

A technical trader may begin viewing the area around 1.1000 as potential support.

Now suppose the same pair repeatedly approaches 1.1200 but struggles to move significantly higher.

The area around 1.1200 might be considered potential resistance.

Support and resistance should generally be thought of as areas rather than guaranteed barriers.

Price can move through them.

A support level does not create an invisible floor.

A resistance level does not create an invisible ceiling.

They simply identify areas where previous market behavior may be relevant.

If price moves decisively through a support or resistance area, traders may describe the movement as a **breakout**.

For example, if a currency pair repeatedly fails to move above a resistance area and then eventually rises through it, some traders may interpret that as evidence of changing market conditions.

But breakouts can fail.

Price may move briefly through a level and then reverse.

This is one reason technical analysis involves uncertainty just like fundamental analysis.

Technical traders may also use indicators.

A **technical indicator** is a mathematical calculation based on market data such as price or, depending on the market and data available, volume.

One common example is a **moving average**, which smooths price information over a selected number of periods.

Rather than focusing on every small movement, a moving average can help traders observe the broader direction of price.

Other indicators attempt to measure momentum, volatility, or other aspects of market behavior.

Beginners can easily become overwhelmed by indicators.

A chart may contain several moving averages, oscillators, lines, signals, and other tools until the actual price becomes difficult to see.

More indicators do not necessarily produce better analysis.

Several indicators may even be measuring similar aspects of the same price data.

The purpose of technical analysis is not to cover a chart with as many tools as possible.

It is to create a consistent framework for interpreting market behavior.

Technical analysis also does not explain why a currency must move.

A chart may show that EUR/USD is trending upward.

Fundamental analysis might help investigate the economic conditions contributing to that movement.

The two approaches therefore do not necessarily need to compete with each other.

Some traders use one primarily.

Others combine them.

Combining Market Analysis With a Trading Plan

Analysis becomes more useful when it is connected to a structured trading process.

A trader can spend hours studying economic reports and charts but still make inconsistent decisions if there is no plan governing how that information will be used.

A **trading plan** is a predefined framework describing how a trader intends to approach the market.

The exact details can differ considerably between traders, but a plan may address questions such as:

Which currency pairs will I trade?

When will I trade?

What conditions must exist before I consider entering?

What type of analysis will I use?

How will I determine my position size?

Where will I exit if the trade moves against me?

Where might I take a profit?

How much am I willing to risk?

What situations will cause me to avoid trading?

These decisions are easier to make before money is at risk.

Once a trade is open, emotions can influence judgment.

A trader may become afraid of taking a loss.

Another may become excited by a rapidly growing profit.

Someone who has just lost several trades may become desperate to recover the money.

A trading plan provides a reference point established before those emotions appear.

Some traders combine fundamental and technical analysis within that plan.

Fundamental analysis might help determine the broader economic environment.

Technical analysis might then help identify potential entry and exit areas.

Consider a simplified hypothetical example.

A trader believes economic conditions are becoming relatively more supportive of Currency A than Currency B.

The central bank behind Currency A is expected to maintain tighter monetary policy, while economic conditions behind Currency B are weakening.

That creates a fundamental view.

The trader does not immediately enter a position.

Instead, the trader examines the price chart.

The currency pair is already moving in the expected direction, but the price has become highly volatile and is far from an area the trader considers suitable for entry.

The trader waits.

Later, price returns toward a previously identified area of support.

The trader reassesses the economic view and determines that the fundamental conditions have not materially changed.

The trader may then consider whether the technical setup fits the trading plan.

This is only an example of how different forms of analysis can be organized.

It is not a formula guaranteeing a profitable trade.

Another trader might use technical analysis almost exclusively.

Another might place greater emphasis on macroeconomic conditions.

What matters is consistency.

A trader should understand why a position is being considered rather than entering because a price is moving quickly or because someone online said a currency was about to rise.

A plan can also identify circumstances in which no trade should be taken.

This is important because beginners sometimes assume successful trading requires constant activity.

It does not.

Overtrading occurs when a trader places excessive or unnecessary trades, often because of boredom, emotional reactions, a desire to recover losses, or the belief that every market movement must be captured.

Every trade introduces potential risk and costs.

Trading more frequently does not automatically create greater profitability.

A plan can help establish conditions that must exist before a trade is considered.

If those conditions are absent, doing nothing can be a legitimate decision.

Traders may also benefit from maintaining a **trading journal**.

A trading journal records information about trading decisions and outcomes.

A journal might include the currency pair, entry and exit, position size, reason for the trade, market conditions, amount risked, outcome, and observations about the trader's decision-making.

The purpose is not merely to keep a list of profits and losses.

It can help identify patterns.

Perhaps a trader performs reasonably well during planned trades but consistently loses money when entering impulsively after major news.

Perhaps losses become larger after several winning trades because the trader becomes overconfident.

Perhaps a particular strategy appears successful in trending markets but performs poorly when prices are moving sideways.

Without records, these patterns can be difficult to recognize.

A trading journal can turn individual trades into information that can be reviewed.

The trader can then ask whether the trading process is actually being followed.

This distinction between process and outcome is important.

A profitable trade is not automatically a good decision.

A trader can ignore risk controls, enter impulsively, and still make money because the market happens to move favorably.

Likewise, a losing trade is not automatically evidence of a poor process.

A trader can follow a carefully considered plan and still experience a loss because uncertainty cannot be removed from financial markets.

Over time, the goal is to evaluate whether the decision-making process is consistent, controlled, and sustainable.

That is where market analysis becomes most useful.

Fundamental and technical analysis are not meant to eliminate uncertainty.

They provide ways to organize information before making decisions within that uncertainty.

Last Thoughts

Forex market analysis gives traders a structured way to evaluate potential opportunities rather than reacting randomly to price movements. Fundamental analysis focuses on economic conditions, central banks, interest rates, and market expectations, while technical analysis examines price behavior through concepts such as trends, support, resistance, breakouts, and indicators. Traders can use these approaches separately or combine them within a trading plan that establishes when they will consider entering, how they will manage positions, and when they will stay out of the market entirely. A trading journal can provide another layer of discipline by helping traders review their decisions rather than focusing only on individual profits and losses. Analysis can improve the structure behind a trading decision, but it cannot remove uncertainty. In the next chapter, we will focus directly on managing that uncertainty by examining position sizing, common beginner mistakes, trading discipline, realistic expectations, and the development of a sustainable trading routine.

Chapter 6: Forex Risk Management and Beginner Trading Practices

Forex trading involves uncertainty. No amount of market analysis can guarantee that a currency pair will move in the direction a trader expects, which makes managing potential losses just as important as identifying potential opportunities. Position size, leverage, stop placement, trading frequency, and emotional decision-making can all influence how much risk a trader ultimately takes. Beginners should therefore think about risk management as part of the trading process rather than something considered only after a trade begins losing money. Developing realistic expectations and consistent trading habits can help create a more disciplined approach to participating in the forex market.

Position Sizing and Managing Trading Risk

Position sizing was introduced earlier as the amount of market exposure represented by a trade.

Now we can examine how traders can connect position size directly to risk.

One of the most important distinctions in forex trading is the difference between **position size** and the amount of money a trader is actually prepared to lose.

A large position does not necessarily mean the trader intends to lose the entire value of that position.

Instead, a trader may determine an acceptable loss first and then select a position size based on the distance between the entry price and the planned exit.

This approach is sometimes described as **risk-based position sizing**.

Consider a simplified example.

Suppose a trader has a $5,000 trading account.

Before entering a particular trade, the trader decides that the maximum planned loss on the position will be $50.

The trader then identifies an entry price and a stop-loss level.

Suppose the distance between those prices is 25 pips.

The trader can use that information to determine a position size where a 25-pip adverse movement corresponds to approximately $50, before accounting for potential slippage and other trading costs.

The calculation begins with the risk rather than the desired profit.

That distinction matters.

A beginner might otherwise look at a potential trade and think:

"How large should my position be if I want to make $500?"

Risk-based thinking asks a different question:

"How large can this position be while keeping the planned loss within an amount I am prepared to accept?"

That change in perspective can discourage excessive position sizes.

Another concept traders may use is **risk per trade**, which refers to the portion of trading capital a trader is willing to expose to a planned loss on one position.

There is no universal percentage that is appropriate for every trader.

Account size, experience, strategy, financial circumstances, trading product, and personal risk tolerance can all affect the decision.

What matters is recognizing that risk should be considered before the trade is entered.

Suppose a trader repeatedly risks a very large percentage of the account on individual trades.

A relatively small sequence of losses can cause substantial damage.

Imagine a trader loses half of an account.

As discussed earlier, a 50 percent loss requires a 100 percent gain on the remaining capital simply to return to the original account value.

Preventing severe losses can therefore be mathematically important to long-term survival.

Traders should also consider **total account exposure**.

A trader might believe each individual position is reasonably sized while overlooking the combined risk created by several open positions.

Suppose a trader buys EUR/USD, GBP/USD, and AUD/USD at the same time.

These are technically three different currency pairs.

But each position may contain meaningful exposure to the U.S. dollar.

If the dollar moves sharply in an unexpected direction, all three trades could potentially be affected simultaneously.

This creates **correlated exposure**, where multiple positions can respond to similar market forces.

Diversifying across several currency pairs does not necessarily mean the risks are independent.

A trader should therefore consider the portfolio of open positions rather than evaluating each trade entirely in isolation.

Leverage adds another layer.

A broker may allow a trader to control substantial exposure relative to the account balance.

That does not mean the trader needs to use all available leverage.

Available leverage determines what may be possible under the account's trading conditions.

Risk management determines what exposure the trader decides is acceptable.

These are very different concepts.

Stop-loss placement also matters.

A stop should not be selected only because it creates the desired monetary risk.

The trader should first determine where the trading idea would reasonably be considered invalid according to the strategy being used.

Position size can then be adjusted to fit the intended monetary risk.

Suppose a trader decides that a stop logically needs to be 50 pips from the entry.

If that distance creates too much financial risk at the planned position size, the solution does not necessarily need to be moving the stop closer.

The trader could reduce the position size.

This allows the market room required by the trading plan while controlling the potential monetary loss.

Even then, stop-loss orders cannot guarantee an exact maximum loss in every situation.

Slippage, rapid price movements, gaps, and unusual market conditions can result in execution beyond the intended stop price.

Risk management reduces and structures exposure.

It does not eliminate market risk.

That is why traders should avoid risking money they cannot afford to lose.

Trading capital should be considered within the trader's broader financial circumstances rather than as money that must produce a particular return.

When money needed for rent, bills, debt payments, emergencies, or other essential expenses is placed at risk, trading decisions can become financially and emotionally dangerous.

Managing trading risk begins before the order reaches the market.

Common Forex Trading Mistakes to Avoid

Beginners can make mistakes even after understanding the mechanics of forex.

Some problems arise because of limited knowledge.

Others occur because emotions interfere with knowledge the trader already has.

One common mistake is **overleveraging**.

Overleveraging occurs when a trader takes excessive market exposure relative to available capital.

Because forex prices can move in relatively small increments, beginners may be tempted to increase leverage to make those movements financially significant.

The problem is that leverage magnifies unfavorable movements too.

A position that appears manageable during calm conditions can produce a substantial loss when volatility increases.

Another mistake is trading without a predetermined risk level.

A trader enters a position expecting it to move favorably.

It moves against them.

Instead of closing according to a plan, the trader waits.

The loss increases.

The trader then decides that closing would make the loss "real," so they continue holding.

Eventually, the position becomes far larger than the trader originally intended.

This is sometimes associated with **loss aversion**, the tendency for people to experience the pain of losses strongly enough that it affects their decision-making.

A trader may avoid accepting a manageable loss because doing so feels uncomfortable.

Ironically, that attempt to avoid the emotional discomfort of a small loss can sometimes create a much larger one.

Moving a stop farther away after a trade begins losing can create a similar problem.

If the original stop represented the point at which the trading idea was considered invalid, changing it simply because the trader does not want to lose undermines the original risk plan.

Another common problem is **revenge trading**.

Revenge trading occurs when someone begins making increasingly emotional or aggressive trading decisions in an attempt to quickly recover a previous loss.

Imagine a trader loses $100.

Frustrated, the trader immediately opens a larger position.

That trade loses too.

Now the trader feels an even stronger need to recover the money.

The next position becomes larger again.

At this point, the trader is no longer following a market analysis process.

The objective has shifted from making a reasoned decision to emotionally undoing the previous loss.

Markets have no obligation to provide that opportunity.

Losses can therefore compound rapidly.

Overtrading, introduced in the previous chapter, can develop for similar reasons.

A trader may feel that being active means being productive.

Every small price movement starts to look like an opportunity.

Positions are opened without meeting the conditions established in the trading plan.

Transaction costs accumulate.

Decision quality can deteriorate.

Sometimes the appropriate trading decision is simply not to trade.

Another mistake is **chasing the market**.

Suppose a currency pair suddenly rises after an economic announcement.

A beginner sees the movement and becomes afraid of missing an opportunity.

The trader enters after much of the move has already occurred.

The market then reverses.

The decision was driven primarily by fear of missing out rather than a planned entry.

Rapid price movement can create psychological pressure because it makes traders feel they must act immediately.

A trading plan can help reduce that pressure by defining what conditions are required before entering.

Beginners may also rely too heavily on other people's trading ideas.

Social media, forums, online groups, videos, and trading communities can contain predictions about which currencies will rise or fall.

Following another person's trade without understanding the reasoning creates several problems.

You may not know their entry price.

You may not know their position size.

You may not know when they plan to exit.

You may not know how much they are willing to lose.

You may not even know whether the person actually placed the trade they are promoting.

Even when another trader's analysis is legitimate, their financial circumstances and risk tolerance may be completely different from yours.

Learning to evaluate information independently is therefore an important beginner skill.

Another mistake is constantly changing strategies.

A trader tries one approach.

After three losing trades, it is abandoned.

The trader finds another strategy online.

That strategy experiences several losses.

It is abandoned too.

Eventually, the trader has tested many approaches without collecting enough consistent information to understand any of them.

This is sometimes called **strategy hopping**.

Trading strategies need to be evaluated over meaningful samples rather than judged solely by a handful of outcomes.

No legitimate strategy eliminates losing trades.

A method can experience a sequence of losses and still potentially have positive characteristics over a larger sample.

Likewise, several profitable trades do not prove that a strategy is reliable.

Beginners should be cautious about drawing large conclusions from small amounts of experience.

Building Discipline, Realistic Expectations, and a Trading Routine

Forex trading is sometimes presented as a way to produce rapid income from a laptop or phone.

That image can create unrealistic expectations before a beginner even learns what a currency pair is.

A more sustainable approach begins by accepting that trading performance is uncertain.

There is no guaranteed daily profit.

There is no requirement that the market provide a profitable opportunity every day.

There is no strategy that wins every trade.

A trader may experience winning periods and losing periods.

This makes **trading discipline** important.

Trading discipline means consistently following a defined decision-making and risk-management process even when emotions create pressure to do something different.

Discipline becomes particularly difficult after both losses and gains.

After a loss, the trader may want to recover money immediately.

After several wins, the trader may become overconfident.

Both situations can lead to excessive risk.

A routine can provide structure around these emotional changes.

A **trading routine** is a repeatable process used to prepare for, execute, and review trading decisions.

A beginner's routine does not need to be complicated.

Before trading, the trader might review scheduled economic events.

Major central bank announcements, inflation reports, employment data, and other important releases can create unusual volatility.

The trader can then review the currency pairs being followed.

What is the broader market environment?

Are prices trending or ranging?

Are important support or resistance areas nearby?

Does the setup meet the conditions established in the trading plan?

If a potential trade exists, the trader can calculate the risk before entering.

What is the entry?

Where is the planned stop?

What position size fits the intended risk?

What trading costs may apply?

Is the potential trade consistent with the plan?

If those questions cannot be answered, the trader may not be ready to enter.

The routine can continue after the trade.

The trader can record the position in a trading journal.

Instead of documenting only whether the trade won or lost, the trader can record why it was taken and whether the plan was followed.

This allows for **trade review**, the process of examining previous trades to evaluate both outcomes and decision-making.

Suppose a trader reviews 50 trades.

Twenty-five were profitable.

Twenty-five lost money.

Simply knowing the number of winners and losers is not enough.

How large were the average wins?

How large were the average losses?

Were profitable trades managed differently?

Did losses become larger when the trader ignored stops?

Did performance change around major economic announcements?

Were certain trades entered outside the plan?

These questions can reveal whether the trading process is working as intended.

A useful concept for evaluating a strategy over many trades is **expectancy**.

Trading expectancy describes the average amount a strategy might be expected to gain or lose per trade over a sufficiently meaningful sample based on its historical win rate and the average size of wins and losses.

A trader does not necessarily need to win most trades to have positive historical expectancy.

Suppose a strategy wins 40 percent of the time but its average winning trade is significantly larger than its average losing trade.

The combination could still produce a positive result over a sufficiently large sample.

The opposite can also occur.

A trader might win 70 percent of trades but experience occasional losses so large that they erase many previous gains.

This is why win rate alone does not describe trading performance.

Risk, reward, costs, consistency, and the size of losses all matter.

Beginners should also separate trading goals from financial pressure.

A goal such as "I must make $200 today" can encourage unnecessary trades because the trader is attempting to force the market to satisfy a personal income requirement.

The market does not know the trader's target.

There may be no appropriate opportunity that day.

A process-oriented goal is different.

The trader might aim to follow the trading plan, remain within predetermined risk limits, record every trade, and avoid impulsive entries.

Those actions are within the trader's control.

The market's outcome is not.

This is one reason **process goals** can be useful.

They focus attention on behavior rather than demanding a particular short-term financial result.

Forex trading should also be evaluated honestly over time.

If a trader is consistently losing money, repeatedly breaking risk rules, or finding that trading creates pressure to risk increasingly larger amounts, simply continuing to trade more aggressively is not a solution.

Reducing position sizes, returning to simulated trading, reviewing the strategy, or stopping live trading entirely can all be reasonable decisions.

Choosing not to trade is always an available option.

The objective of developing discipline is not to transform uncertainty into certainty.

It is to create a process that acknowledges uncertainty before money is placed at risk.

Last Thoughts

Forex risk management begins with accepting that losing trades cannot be eliminated. Position sizing, leverage control, stop-loss planning, and awareness of total account exposure can help determine how damaging an unsuccessful trade may become. Beginners should also recognize behavioral risks such as overleveraging, revenge trading, chasing price movements, overtrading, and abandoning strategies based on a small number of results. A structured trading routine, realistic expectations, consistent recordkeeping, and regular trade review can provide greater discipline, but none of these practices guarantees profitability. The purpose of risk management is not to make forex trading safe or predictable. It is to help traders define and control the risks they choose to take while recognizing that preserving capital and choosing not to trade can be just as important as identifying the next potential opportunity.

Last Thoughts

Learning how forex and currency trading works is different from learning how to predict what a currency will do next. Throughout this book, we have focused on building the foundation first: understanding the foreign exchange market, reading currency pairs, interpreting exchange rates, measuring price movements, understanding leverage and margin, placing orders, analyzing markets, and managing risk. These concepts give beginners a clearer picture of what actually happens when a forex position is opened and why the potential for profit always comes with the possibility of loss. As you continue learning, the goal should not be to eliminate uncertainty, but to become more informed about the market, more deliberate about the risks you take, and more disciplined in the decisions you make.

Understanding Forex Before Risking Money

Forex trading can appear deceptively simple from the outside.

A trading platform may display a chart, two prices, and buttons allowing you to buy or sell.

The technical act of placing a trade may take only seconds.

Understanding the financial decision behind that trade requires considerably more knowledge.

You need to know which currencies you are trading.

You need to understand how the currency pair is quoted.

You need to know how much market exposure the position creates.

You need to understand how much each price movement could be worth.

You need to recognize the costs involved in entering, maintaining, and exiting the position.

Most importantly, you need to understand how much you could lose.

This is why beginners should avoid treating the ability to place a trade as evidence that they are prepared to trade.

Modern trading platforms can make market access easy.

They cannot make market risk disappear.

The concepts throughout this book provide a foundation for understanding what is happening behind the buttons on the screen.

When you see EUR/USD quoted at a particular exchange rate, you now know that the price represents the value of the euro relative to the U.S. dollar.

When the pair rises, you understand what that means for the relationship between the base and quote currencies.

When a platform displays a bid and ask price, you understand that the difference creates a spread.

When someone discusses a 50-pip movement, you know that the monetary significance of those pips depends on position size.

When a broker offers leverage, you understand that the trader may be controlling substantially more market exposure than the capital committed as margin.

That final point deserves particular attention.

Leverage can make forex trading appear more accessible because a trader does not necessarily need enough capital to fully fund the value of a leveraged position.

But reducing the amount of capital required to establish the position does not reduce the exposure created by that position.

The market moves against the entire position.

This is why understanding leverage before using it is essential.

The same principle applies to trading orders.

A stop-loss order can help define an intended exit, but it does not eliminate the possibility of loss or guarantee an exact execution price under every market condition.

A take-profit order can automatically close a favorable position, but it cannot guarantee that the market will reach the target.

A limit order can help control the price at which a trader wants to transact, but the trade may never be executed.

Every trading tool has a purpose and limitations.

Understanding both is part of becoming an informed market participant.

Beginners should also recognize that there is nothing wrong with spending substantial time learning without trading real money.

Watching currency pairs can be educational.

Following economic releases can help you observe how markets respond to new information.

Practicing order entry through a demo account can help you become familiar with the mechanics of a trading platform.

Reviewing hypothetical trades can help you practice calculating risk.

Learning does not require immediate financial exposure.

There will always be another currency movement.

Feeling pressured to participate immediately can encourage beginners to take risks before they understand them.

Forex should be approached as a financial market first and a trading opportunity second.

The more clearly you understand what you are trading, the better prepared you are to decide whether taking that risk makes sense for you.

Continuing Your Currency Trading Education

Finishing a beginner guide should not be treated as the end of your forex education.

It should provide a foundation for deciding what you need to learn next.

One area worth continuing to study is market analysis.

We introduced fundamental and technical analysis in this book, but both subjects extend far beyond the introductory concepts covered here.

Fundamental analysis can lead into deeper study of inflation, employment, economic growth, central banking, monetary policy, international trade, and capital flows.

These topics can help explain some of the economic forces influencing currencies.

Technical analysis can lead into deeper study of market structure, trends, price behavior, volatility, chart patterns, and different approaches to identifying potential entries and exits.

Neither area needs to be learned all at once.

A beginner can gradually build knowledge while observing how the concepts behave in actual markets.

Risk management deserves continued study as well.

Understanding that position size matters is the beginning.

Learning how position size interacts with stop distance, pip value, total account exposure, leverage, and multiple simultaneous trades provides a deeper understanding of trading risk.

The more you study these relationships, the easier it becomes to recognize why two traders can place similar trades while taking dramatically different amounts of financial risk.

You can also continue learning about the specific currency pairs you are interested in following.

Every currency represents an economy.

That economy has a central bank.

It has interest rates.

It has economic strengths and weaknesses.

It may depend heavily on particular industries, exports, commodities, trading partners, or sources of investment.

Understanding the currencies themselves can add context that a price chart alone cannot provide.

Beginners may find it useful to focus on a limited number of currency pairs initially rather than attempting to follow every available market.

This can make it easier to become familiar with the economic information, trading sessions, volatility, and price behavior associated with those currencies.

Continued education should also involve learning how to evaluate information critically.

Forex is surrounded by educational material, market commentary, trading signals, strategies, social media content, courses, communities, and promotional claims.

The quality of that information varies enormously.

A polished presentation does not prove that a strategy works.

A screenshot of a profitable trade does not reveal someone's complete trading record.

A large social media following does not guarantee expertise.

A trader showing several winning positions may not show the losing positions that occurred between them.

This makes **due diligence** important.

Due diligence means taking reasonable steps to investigate and evaluate information before relying on it.

When encountering a trading claim, ask what evidence supports it.

When reviewing a strategy, consider whether costs and losing trades are included.

When evaluating a broker or trading provider, investigate its regulatory status, fees, trading conditions, withdrawal policies, and other relevant terms.

When someone promises unusually consistent or guaranteed returns, approach the claim with caution.

You should also continue learning through your own records.

A trading journal can become increasingly valuable as the number of observed or completed trades grows.

Over time, you can review whether your actual behavior matches your intended process.

You may discover that certain mistakes repeatedly appear.

You may notice that you trade differently after a loss.

You may find that certain market conditions do not fit your approach.

Education therefore does not come only from books or courses.

It can also come from systematically reviewing your own decisions.

The objective is not to collect endless amounts of forex information.

It is to gradually develop a better understanding of the information that is relevant to the decisions you make.

Becoming a More Informed and Disciplined Trader

Trading discipline is not something a person develops simply by deciding to "be disciplined."

It develops through repeated behaviors.

A trader establishes rules.

The trader follows them.

The results are recorded.

The decisions are reviewed.

Mistakes are identified.

The process is adjusted when appropriate.

Then it is repeated.

This process may sound less exciting than searching for the next major currency movement, but consistency is an important part of managing trading risk.

One useful distinction is between what the trader can control and what the trader cannot control.

You cannot control where EUR/USD trades tomorrow.

You cannot control what a central bank announces.

You cannot control whether an economic report surprises the market.

You cannot control how millions of other market participants respond to new information.

You can control whether you enter a trade.

You can control the position size you choose.

You can decide how much leverage you use.

You can establish an intended risk level.

You can decide whether a potential setup meets your trading plan.

You can choose whether to chase a market that has already moved.

You can decide whether to stop trading after emotions begin affecting your judgment.

Focusing on these controllable decisions can help shift attention away from the idea that successful trading requires correctly predicting every market movement.

It also makes it easier to evaluate your performance.

Suppose you follow your trading plan carefully and a trade loses money.

The outcome is disappointing, but the loss alone does not necessarily mean the decision-making process was poor.

Now suppose you ignore your plan, take an oversized position, and make a substantial profit.

The financial outcome is positive, but the process may still have been dangerous.

This distinction is important because markets can sometimes reward poor decisions in the short term.

A trader can take excessive risk and win.

That win can create overconfidence.

The trader takes even more risk on the next position.

Eventually, a large adverse movement can expose how dangerous the original behavior was.

Discipline means evaluating the quality of the decision rather than allowing one profitable outcome to justify unnecessary risk.

It also means accepting that losses will occur.

Trying to avoid every losing trade can create harmful behavior.

A trader may refuse to close a losing position.

Stops may be moved.

Risk may be increased.

Another trade may be opened in an attempt to recover the loss.

These behaviors can transform an ordinary trading loss into a much larger problem.

A planned loss should not automatically be viewed as a failure.

If the position remained within predetermined risk limits and the trading process was followed, the loss may simply represent one of the uncertain outcomes inherent in trading.

This is where realistic expectations become valuable.

Forex trading does not need to produce income every day.

A trader does not need to participate in every market movement.

Missing a profitable trade does not create a financial loss.

Choosing not to trade when conditions do not fit your plan can be a disciplined decision.

Stepping away after recognizing emotional decision-making can also be a disciplined decision.

Reducing position size when uncertainty is unusually high can be a disciplined decision.

Returning to simulated trading while developing a new approach can be a disciplined decision.

Sometimes the most important trading decisions involve not placing a trade at all.

Becoming more informed does not mean becoming fearless.

Risk deserves respect.

It also does not mean becoming certain.

Uncertainty remains part of every trade.

The goal is to understand the market well enough that when you decide to participate, you understand what you are trading, why you are trading it, what could cause the idea to fail, and how much you are prepared to risk if it does.

That is a very different approach from simply pressing buy or sell and hoping the market moves in your favor.

Last Thoughts

Forex and currency trading brings together exchange rates, global financial markets, currency pairs, pips, spreads, position sizes, leverage, margin, trading orders, market analysis, and risk management. Understanding these concepts does not guarantee profitable trading, but it can help remove some of the confusion surrounding what happens when a forex position is opened and managed. As you continue learning, focus on understanding the risks as carefully as you study potential opportunities. Build knowledge gradually, evaluate information critically, practice disciplined decision-making, and recognize that protecting your capital matters alongside pursuing potential returns. The foreign exchange market will continue moving whether you participate in a particular trade or not. Becoming a more informed trader means learning when and how to participate, while also being willing to recognize when the better decision is not to trade at all.

About the Author

Roggie "Raj" Clark is an entrepreneur and a 10-year marketing professional with a proven track record in e-commerce and digital business growth. Having built and managed successful online stores with thousands of sales and consulted for numerous marketing clients, Roggie has mastered the intricacies of online marketing, branding, and consumer behavior. He has also written several popular books on digital marketing, SEO (search engine optimization), and programming (HTML, CSS, and JavaScript).

As a former marketing manager at a fintech company—a role he secured through his own marketing and financial expertise—Roggie gained firsthand experience in financial strategy and wealth-building. This journey inspired him to share insights with amateur investors, helping them save money, make smarter financial decisions, and build long-term wealth. Raj currently lives in Maryland with his sister and niece.

www.ingramcontent.com/pod-product-compliance
Lightning Source LLC
LaVergne TN
LVHW050822061126
851857LV00012B/923
* 9 7 9 8 2 5 6 2 9 2 1 5 7 *